A Beginner's Guide to
Angelfish

Written by
Gene Wolfsheimer

D0946802

Contents

1.
Introduction

As a hobby, keeping aquaria to house various fishes and aquatic animals is a fairly old one. It is second only to photography as man's favorite avocation.

The beauty and grace of the angelfish have made it one of the most popular of all tropicals. Photo by A. Roth.

Amongst our aquarium fishes there have always been particular favorites, and these have changed as new species were introduced. But when the angelfish made its appearance it became "number one on the hit parade". It has remained so to this day. Nicknamed the "king of the aquarium", never was a title so rightly deserved. If anyone cares to dispute this the final argument is the volume of fish sales. Angelfish outsell most other tropicals by far.

What is the reason for this dominance? Just a few minutes of watching these fish will not only give the answer, but make you a convert if you are not already one of the cult.

The "king" is, indeed, regal. Besides having a different appearance from almost all other fishes, he swims gracefully about without awkwardness or eccentricity. When in a school of his own kind, the whole pack turns and flows together like a flock of sheep grazing on a hillside. The angelfish is alert, inquisitive, and for a fish...intelli-

Cichlasoma festivum, *like the angelfish a member of the family Cichlidae, also makes a good aquarium fish. Photo by R. Zukal.*

Magnificent marbleized angelfish. Photo by A. Roth.

gent. The Cichlidae, of which the angel is a member, have parental instincts such as few other fishes in the hobby can display. Certain species, sometimes kept as a single display specimen, are treated as house pets and given special attention, including hand-feeding and petting.

Habitat

South America is the home of the angelfish; more specifically, Brazil, parts of Guiana, and even as far as Peru and East Ecuador, including the basin of the vast Amazon river and its tributaries. It is said that this fish is often found in the company of another cichlid kept in the hobby, *Cichlasoma festivum*.

Collectors tell of finding the angel in slow-moving streams often carpeted heavily with reed-like growths and heavy algae. Again, they are known to inhabit extensive flooded areas with rocky surroundings. In either case it seems obvious that they are specifically constructed to move through such areas easily. Pursued by a predacious foe, they often manage to escape because of their peculiarly individualistic bodies and the matching surrounding terrain.

Taxonomy

To date, three species of *Pterophyllum,* or angelfish, are recognized, not necessarily by sight, but because they have been identified scientifically. They include: *P. scalare, P. eimekei* and *P. altum.*

Angelfish were originally collected well over 100 years ago and have borne a number of synonymous identifications: *Pterophyllum scalare,* Lichtenstein, 1823; *Platax scalaris* Cuvier & Valenciennes, 1831; *Pterophyllum scalare* Heckel, 1840: Gunther, 1862; Steindachner, 1875; Pellegrin, 1902; Regan, 1905; ? *Plataxoides dumerilii* Castelnau, 1855; *Pterophyllum altum* Pellegrin, 1902; *Pterophyllum eimekei* Ahl, 1928.

In 1911 a few living specimens of *Pterophyllum scalare* were introduced in Europe. Innes states in his book *Exotic Aquarium Fishes* that *Pterophyllum* means "winged leaf", and *scalare,* "like a flight of stairs, referring to the dorsal fin". It is interesting to note that the word "angelfish" and the name "scalare" are used interchangeably. The first edition of Innes' book was printed in 1935 and certain of the text concerning angelfish remains unchanged.

Twenty years ago the word *"scalare"* was synonymous with "angelfish". A fish dealer who was asked for a *scalare* immediately put his net into his angelfish aquarium. Today, this term is seldom used. In those days *the* angelfish was *Pterophyllum scalare,* or so scientists and illustrators would have us believe. This species is recorded as the largest of the genus *Pterophyllum,* measuring about six inches in length and ten to eleven inches high. *P. eimekei* is somewhat smaller, being about four inches in length and eight to nine inches in height. *P. altum* has been recorded as approximately the same size as *eimekei.* It has but recently been imported from its native haunt and still remains unbred.

Present-day tank-raised angelfish are of uncertain ancestry. *Scalare* and *eimekei* are supposed to have been cross-bred and their progeny proved fertile and capable of

An individual Pterophyllum altum, *an angelfish species that is not often seen in the aquarium trade. Photo by Dr. Herbert R. Axelrod.*

reproducing. Speculation exists suggesting that both of these "species" are, in effect, sub-species. The crossing of two distinct species almost without exception results in infertile offspring incapable of reproducing. On the other hand, the crossing of two known sub-species usually produces fertile young. Needless to say, the genus *Pterophyllum* could stand a great deal more taxonomic research.

Angelfish are very tall and thin, and their height is emphasized by their huge sweeping dorsal, ventral and anal fins. These make the fish about one and a half times as tall as it is long. Just as a tall tree or a skyscraper has its own majesty, so has an angelfish in an aquarium full of fishes of all kinds.

The ventral fins are developed into long threadlike appendages and curve into a beautiful sweeping arc, especially when the fish is in motion. Unlike the feeler-like ventrals of certain air-breathing fishes, these fins are not used as sensory organs.

Closeup of the front of an angelfish, showing pronouncedly sharp angulation of the "forehead." Photo by Dr. Herbert R. Axelrod.

Note the redness of the eyes of this spawning marble angelfish. Photo by H. J. Richter.

The iris of the eye is usually a rich red color, and although certain changes have occurred in the appearance of the angel, due to the breeding of new strains, the color seems to remain constant and is most attractive.

Both the dorsal and anal fins are basically the same shape. On normal specimens the end of the dorsal is usually somewhat rounded, while the tip of the anal fin becomes filamentous and pointed.

The upward-slanted mouth emerges at the end of a sharply-pointed snout. It is only the snout that keeps the body from being almost symmetrically rounded.

The fish accepted in the hobby as the standard common angelfish is often referred to as the "silver" angel. Silver it is, but basically this color runs the gamut from a silver-white through grayish to an almost olive-green in its more subtle shadings. The dorsal and anal fins have a bluish-silver hue that lightens towards their extremities. Four vertical black bars line the body. One runs through the eye. A second traverses the body from the dorsal point to the vent. The third is the largest, running down the dorsal, through the body and on down into the anal fin. The last bar darkens the end of the body at the base of the tail. Later in this book angelfish variations, both in color and finnage, will be discussed. The body of the angelfish is covered by small ctenoid scales. The pectorals are colorless.

As these fish get older, and they are known to live more than eight years, they sometimes develop a protuberant forehead. This is often more pronounced on known males than females.

The present-day size of the angelfish varies somewhat, depending upon the regulatory processes that control the growth of all fishes. These include food, swimming space and water conditions.

Veiltail angelfish of the normal silver pattern. Photo by A. Roth.

2.
Maintenance

Feeding

As with almost all the cichlids, the angelfish is a decided carnivore. It requires a high protein diet to properly sustain itself. It is also a predatory fish and prefers to stalk its prey and eat it alive. It will eat and relish most living

Healthy angelfish have good appetites and eagerly await the coming of their owner with food—here they wait expectantly to see what's going to come their way.

foods recommended for tropical fishes, including daphnia, mosquito larvae, bite-sized water crustacea, various worms (either whole or chopped if too large to be eaten whole), live brine shrimp and even drosophila, the wingless fruit fly. Even when stalking small bite-sized living foods, the angel often presents a fierce front, with dorsal and anal very straight and stiff, ventrals parted and pushed forward, and the whole effect augmented by a quick striking action.

Angelfish also relish other fish, and as they grow larger they are quite capable of eating various species of the smaller fishes kept in the hobby. Most angel-keepers can attest to their pets eating baby livebearers, probably discovering this by accident when the absence of newly-dropped livebearers was noticed. The angelfish may have

Living tubifex worms are greatly relished by angelfish. Photo by Michael Gilroy.

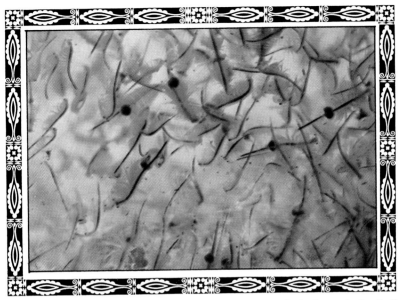

Brine shrimp in its various forms is one of the prime foods for tropicals of all types. Live adult brine shrimp shown here. Photo by Michael Gilroy.

been actually seen stalking and eating their prey. There are some angel-lovers who purposely keep a few breeding livebearers with their large pets so that they can occasionally enjoy a meal of living food. Other fish-keepers dispose of their angels because of their fry-eating habits. The large angels may be replaced by smaller specimens, but often a less predatory species is substituted.

If living foods are not available angelfish can be taught to accept substitutes, including bits of fish or shellfish, scrapings of raw beef or liver, and various frozen varieties of once-living foods. It is probable that the greatest number of angels kept by hobbyists today exist upon the universally accepted dry food. This does keep them alive, but they seldom attain either maximum size or breeding condition. If either dry food or a paste-like substance is used, read the label on the package to make sure that it has a high   protein content.

Swimming space

A fully-grown angelfish is considered to be, by home aquarium standards, a large fish, and with its maximum growth comes its maximum beauty. More than a few authors describing the beauty of the angelfish have written words akin to poetry. For although the angelfish is usually seen in its basic colors of black vertical stripings on its silver-white body, well-conditioned adults have subtle hues of green or blue, and their red eyes become more fiery with their well-being.

An angelfish needs adequate swimming space to grow and prosper. True, little specimens with a body size of a ten-cent piece do quite well in the seven or ten gallon home aquaria, but as they grow so should their home. A year-old angel, raised properly, can attain almost its maximum size of five inches in length and nine to ten inches in

Top: *Veitail angelfish showing the marbleized pattern. Photo by Dr. Herbert R. Axelrod.* **Facing page:** *Graceful angelfish swimming in unison are one of the most beautiful sights the aquarium world has to offer.*

height. At a year it could have been breeding for three or four months. On the other hand, some home aquarium specimens seldom reach half this size in a year. Crowded swimming space, either from an aquarium of a restricted size or from too many other aquarium inhabitants, usually accounts for this.

Water conditions

Angelfish are most undemanding. This must surely be one reason for their popularity. Considered a true tropical fish, their water should be kept at a temperature of 75 degrees. for their comfort and attractiveness. A rise of 4 to 8 degrees can be maintained when breeding them is desired. References describing the angelfish's local waters would indicate that they require a soft, somewhat acid condition. This could have been true with the first as well as present-day imports. However, today's tank-raised specimens have adapted themselves to exist comfortably upon as varied a water chemistry as can be found in the various countries of the world. This is one species that is maintained universally. They thrive and procreate in reasonably hard alkaline water apparently as readily as in their recommended native soft acid conditions.

Today pet shops and aquarium specialty stores sell a wide range of different pre-pared foods that provide enough of a variety to make sure that all of the angel-fish's nutritional requirements are met.

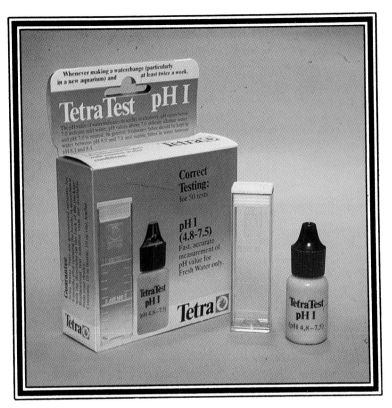

Kits for testing the relative acidity/alkalinity of the aquarium water are available at the pet shops; they're inexpensive and easy to use.

Angels, like many species of fishes, enjoy clean, clear water. The use of an aquarium filter, with or without additional aerator, is recommended. Partial changes of water are extremely beneficial, and are often a deciding factor if the fish are to breed. Their aquarium water should be siphoned out from the bottom to remove settled sediment to a depth of about a fifth to a quarter of the aquarium, and replaced with fresh water of the same temperature, or a degree or two higher. This practice is so beneficial that the results are often immediately noticeable from the actions of the fish. Fins straighten and, after the initial fright from the disturbance is over, colors return. They begin to flirt, fight mock battles with each other, and beg for food.

Hunger strikes are a peculiarity of angelfish. They sometimes just stop eating, and although they will pick at their food or take it in their mouths they refuse to swallow it and spit it out; and they will do this no matter how tempting are the tidbits offered to them. This can be most frustrating for the owner. Not only does he value them as pets and hate to see them off their food; he is wasting both time and money on them, and their actual cash value is decreased.

Several guesses can be made as to why these hunger strikes happen: the fish is perhaps being picked on by some of its angel associates, and after having been chased away from its food for some time has given up trying to get any; it may be physically ill, the cause possibly being an internal parasite, and thus has no desire to eat; or there is a strong possibility that a combination of these factors, plus a general decline in living conditions in the aquarium, has made it listless and disinclined to eat. Most competent authorities seem to agree that partial water changes will prevent this hunger strike from occurring, or if it has, be of great assistance in overcoming the problem.

This wild-caught angelfish is obviously deformed; deformed fishes usually don't live long in the wild. Photo by Dr. Herbert R. Axelrod.

3.
Breeding

Although countless reams of paper have been used to describe the lives and loves of angelfish, seldom is there any detailed account without the author attempting to describe sex differences. With angels, this is not easy. It is true that in many instances the male of the egg-laying

Above: A pair of angelfish tending the eggs they
have laid on the leaf of a Cryptocoryne *plant.*
Photo by H. J. Richter.

It is very difficult to sex angelfish with any degree of certainty outside the actual spawning period, but at spawning time it is easy, because the genital papillae of the sexes are very different; the female's ovipositor is much broader and less pointed than the male's papilla. Photo by H. J. Richter.

species (and angels do lay eggs) is the larger of the sexes. This means very little, however, with angelfish, for often the larger and more robust of a pair will turn out to be the female. Equal size differential between the sexes is totally unimportant as long as they accept each other, and one is capable of laying eggs and the other of fertilizing them.

Knowledgeable fish-breeders prefer to let angels choose their own mates. Most cichlids, given the opportunity to pair up naturally, will respond favorably and choose a mate carefully. Those aquarists who are interested in obtaining breeding pairs of angels should get six or seven young specimens not more than two or three inches high. Adequate housing, proper food, swimming space, and cleanliness will eventually lead to a pairing-off, sometimes when they are nine or ten months old.

This pairing requires close observation on the part of the fish-keeper. It is usually nothing more than two fish taking over one particular area and keeping the other aquarium inhabitants away. Sometimes this area is a corner or even one whole side of the aquarium. Sometimes it is nothing more than a space around a leaf or tall rock or ornament which is chosen as a spawning site.

Some of the more informed aquarists or breeders have certain techniques by which they can more or less reliably choose either sex. The best known of these is the shape and spacing of the lower edge of the body that lies between the long slender trailing ventral fins and the single long anal fin that juts out beneath the fish.

The male fish's body in this area slopes gently downward, almost from the lower jaw to the leading edge of the anal fin, without too definite a change of outline. The female's, on the other hand, has a decided difference, for the outline curves in a circular pattern from the jaw around to the lower center of the body, where it meets the anal fin to make a 90 degrees downward plunge at the anal's leading edge.

Closeup of a leaf almost entirely covered by angelfish eggs. Photo by H. J. Richter.

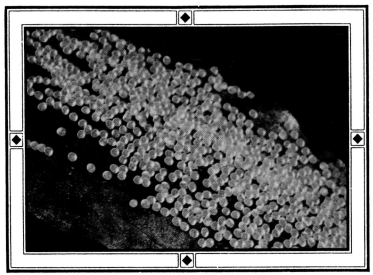

Prior to actual breeding, a female's abdomen has a more rotund appearance, due to the ripened eggs within her, and this is of some aid in sexing these fish.

Angelfish are not too secretive about an impending spawning, but it remains the aquarist's business to note any changes of normal activities that foretell this. First indications include mock battles between the angels. Often these are lip-to-lip tugging arrangements. In this manner they can, by using strength, dominance and determination, choose a suitable mate, one that will stand alongside the other and share the care of their future offspring.

When the testing is finally over, a pair will then keep company in harmony and reserve their own particular area. This could be a future spawning site. If it is conve-

Below and facing page: Before any eggs are laid the parents carefully inspect and use their mouths to clean the surface of the area that has been chosen as the place for depositing the eggs. Photo by H. J. Richter.

nient, other aquarium inhabitants should be moved out to give the pair a greater sense of security. However, the angels that are paired off can spawn while in with others of their own kind or with mixed species.

Spawning occurs in a typical cichlid fashion, with one exception. Most cichlids (the group of fish to which angels belong) prefer to spawn upon fairly horizontal areas near the bottom or lower half of the aquarium. Angels, and discus too, seem to prefer a more vertical site such as long swordplant leaves or even the glass side of the aquarium. Noticeable too is the height at which they spawn. The spawning location is usually in the upper half of the aquarium.

Just before the actual spawning takes place the pair of angels start picking with their mouths at several locations, possibly to see if they can support the spawning action. At this time, not only is the abdomen of the female somewhat enlarged due to the presence of her eggs, but usually the ovipositor or egg-tube is visible. This tube protrudes from her vent and through it pass the eggs as they are being laid. Sometimes this blunt-edged tube can reach a length of half an inch during the spawning.

The site which has been decided on is scrupulously picked at and cleaned with their mouths, and near the end of this action the female makes test runs with her body over the spot. Her tube rubs gently against it. Eggs are usually forthcoming shortly after this.

After the female has swum over the spawning site, her ovipositor gently releasing a single stream of sticking eggs, the male follows close behind on the same path. He, too, has a breeding tube extending from his vent, but it

The female deposits the adhesive eggs by swimming over the spawning site and attaching the eggs to it by means of her ovipositor. Photo by H. J. Richter.

The eggs are grouped closely instead of strung out loosely. Photo by H. J. Richter.

is much shorter and pointed. Going over the just-laid eggs he releases his invisible milt and fertilized them. These actions are repeated again and again until all the female's eggs are laid in a compact one-layer mass.

The whole act of spawning is quite exciting. During it the fish are particularly alert and keep all intruders a good distance away. Often the nose of the aquarist watching the proceedings close to the glass of the aquarium is threatened. A finger or hand put into the water near the spawning is struck at with little regard for danger to themselves.

When the spawning is over either both fish together, or one or the other alternately, will assume the parental duties necessary to insure a safe hatching. The eggs require attention to keep them clean. One of the parents will hover gently over the eggs with its pectoral fins pumping to keep a current of clean water passing over them. At the same time it will intermittently pick off any detritus that might have settled upon them.

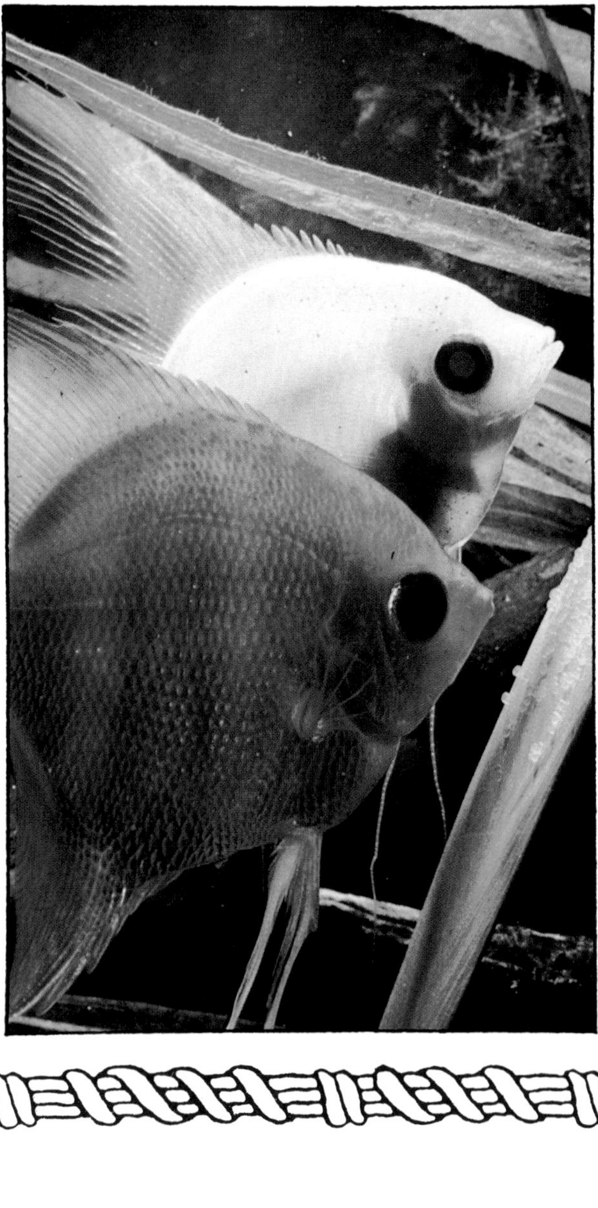

4.
Rearing

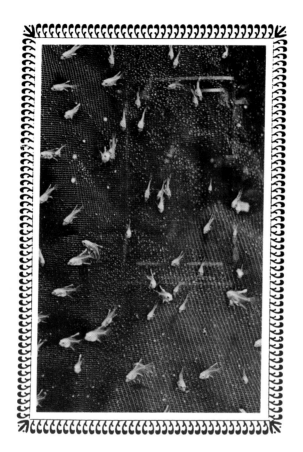

Under normal circumstances cichlid eggs, angelfish included, hatch in approximately three to four days. Then the newly-hatched fry cling, together or singly, on the spawning site by means of a tiny thread attached to their heads. In this manner they wriggle and vibrate for another

*Facing page: The parents remain alertly on guard against any danger that can threaten eggs or fry. **Above:** These golden angel fry are only a few weeks old. Photos by H. J. Richter.*

three to four days before finally rising up to school and swim about looking for food under the guidance and protection of their parents.

During the first period of their free-swimming stage the fry are herded together and bedded down at night on sites which might include the original spawning place, but often they vary. Each is always chosen carefully and usually cleansed by a picking action with the parents' mouths. This moving about instead of maintaining a permanent spot is often employed by most of the cichlid-type fishes. It has caused considerable conjecture on the part of both hobbyists and behavioral scientists. It would seem that the parent fish inherit this precautionary action which is a means of preventing a planned predation of their flock in the dark of night. Any predatory animal, whether a fish or an amphibian, that had "cased" the

The parent angelfish guard the eggs and inspect them constantly, removing any that go bad and become fungused. Photo by H. J. Richter.

THE WORLD'S LARGEST SELECTION OF PET, ANIMAL, AND MUSIC BOOKS.

. Publications publishes more than 900 books covering many hobby aspects (dogs, birds, fish, small animals, music, etc.). Whether you are a beginner or an advanced ist you will find exactly what you're looking for among our complete listing of books. free catalog fill out the form on the other side of this page and mail it today.

CATS . . .

. . . BIRDS . .

. . . ANIMALS . . .

. . . DOGS . . .

FISH . . .

. . . MUSIC . . .

For more than 30 years, *Tropical Fish Hobbyist* has been the source of accurate, up-to-the-minute, and fascinating information on every facet of the aquarium hobby.

Join the more tha 50,000 devoted reade worldwide wh wouldn't mi a sing issu

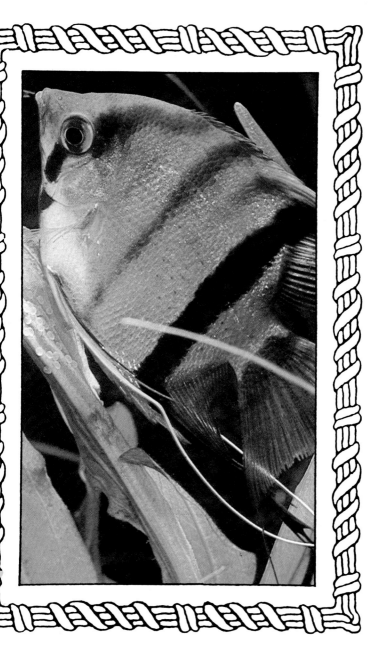

The leaves of broad-leafed plants often are used for the site on which eggs are
deposited, but generally a piece of clean slate or shale, placed in the tank so that
it inclines at an angle against the aquarium glass, will be chosen in preference
to plants. Photo by H. J. Richter.

Parent angelfish surrounded by a cloud of their young. Unfortunately, the sight is not often seen, as most baby angels are taken away from their parents and hatched artificially.

previous night's resting spot would be surprised to find it empty. With their alert vigil during the day and the precautions taken at night, the fry have a better opportunity than many other types of fishes to stay alive and prosper. In this manner the tiny fry, growing slowly at first, start filling out. Before long their little dorsal and anal fins begin to lengthen, typifying their heritage as young "kings".

If the aquarium is a large one a spawning of angels can be brought up with the parents. The sight of parent angelfish, proud and protective, with their young swimming about them, is certainly for the privileged. It doesn't happen too often. Fortunate are the owners of a pair of angelfish who will take proper care of their eggs and raise the young beyond a size where they can be eaten.

Unfortunately, this normal method of spawning is a rare occurrence. For reasons that can only be guessed at, breeding angels in aquaria usually destroy a spawning, and the result is always disappointing for the owner.

During spawning, when the eggs are actually being laid, the male might eat them. Sometimes it will be the female who does this, and sometimes both. One or both parents will start picking at the eggs and apparently acquire a taste for them; and their attempts at cleaning them end with the eggs being eaten.

Another thing that seems to encourage the parents to eat the eggs is the over-stimulation of their protective instincts. Should the fish be disturbed during the breeding or post-spawning attempts to maintain the eggs properly, they will start to eat the spawn. This action seems to have a "before we let something else eat the eggs we'll eat them ourselves" attitude about it. This occurs frequently.

Young angelfish grow quickly if given enough room and the proper foods—and a school of angelfish babies is a welcome sight to any aquarium hobbyist. Photo by H. J. Richter.

It is also interesting to note that, although the eggs of the angelfish are adhesive and stick to the spot where they have been deposited, the fish sometimes brush against them and knock them off. First spawnings for a female are sometimes notoriously poor. She releases the eggs before she is on the site or after she has passed it. If this happens the eggs start dropping to the bottom. One or the other parent will catch them in its mouth and try to blow them on to the spawning site, but not having been properly pushed into place, they seldom stick. After several attempts at this these loose eggs are eaten. This might be another way that the taste for eggs is acquired.

Of all the reasons why spawnings are unsuccessful and eventually eaten, one is far more frustrating than the others. This is when a beautiful, healthy female decides to spawn and does so, but without allowing a male to

One of the angels known as "spotted" angels.

A wild angelfish caught near Humaita, Brazil. Photo by Dr. Herbert R. Axelrod.

fertilize the eggs. She is quite adamant about this and will fight off any attempts by a male to do this. She guards the eggs for awhile, but before long more venturesome inhabitants of the aquarium sidle over and get in some quick bites at the spawning. Seeing her spawning disappearing, the female ends up helping herself to the eggs too.

Artificial techniques

Because the angelfish is so popular in the hobby, and because there is a great demand for them, breeders, whether amateurs or professionals, do their best to breed them in vast quantities. Breeders cannot depend upon the whims of the parent fish to raise their babies and therefore use artificial means to insure success. These techniques are simple and effective.

Black angelfish. Photo by A. Roth.

After the parent fish have spawned, and it has been observed as a normal spawning with proper fertilization by a male, the eggs are removed. They are placed in a small aquarium or non-toxic receptacle that contains sufficient water to cover the eggs for at least a few inches. The water used for this purpose is usually drawn from the breeding aquarium but it can be from other sources, including preconditioned tap water. If it is new water, air should be allowed to bubble through it for a day or two. It should, like any water used for egg-hatching, be of the same temperature as the breeding aquarium. It has been noted, however, that fresh water is often different enough in its chemical make-up to prevent the eggs from hatching.

A mild fungicide such as methylene blue or acriflavine is placed into the water in the hatching container. Both these are available at most aquaria shops as remedies for fungus disease of fish. They can be used in the same dosage recommended to treat fish. Since harmful bacteria in the water often attack the eggs and cause them to fungus, this is a preventative measure. If some of the eggs were not fertilized and do fungus, as sometimes happens, this same fungicide helps to prevent the fungus from spreading and attacking the good eggs.

Professional breeders encourage spawning adult fish to breed on certain objects placed in their aquarium. This facilitates the egg removal, because the spawning can be gently lifted out without damage or disturbance. These objects are generally of a similar shape. The most popular is a long thin piece of slate resting on the bottom and leaning up against the side of the aquarium almost to the surface. Sometimes the lower ends of the slate are mounted in a piece of cement to prevent them falling over. Other objects can be glass or plastic rods, pieces of tall narrow building tile or any firm, reasonably smooth material upon which the fish can stick their eggs. A very good natural spawning site is a tall leaf of a plant. For

Veiltail angelfish showing much more black than is present in the normal silver angelfish; photo by A. Roth.

this reason certain aquatic plants such as swordplants or the larger *Cryptocorynes* are sleected for a breeding angelfish aquarium. Some breeders feel it is important that their fish spawn upon a natural object and will use rubber bands to fasten a large flat leaf, sometimes terrestrial in nature, to a tall flat surface, such as the aforementioned piece of slate. Any of these spawning sites is removable and can be placed in the hatching aquarium. It should be sufficiently covered by water. If the eggs were spawned upon a leaf then the leaf must be removed from the parent plant and put in the hatching aquarium, and weighted down by a small stone or a piece of lead foil.

Besides the fungicide in the water, the natural fanning motion done by the pectoral fin of the parents is replaced by a current of air from an airstone near the eggs.

The sedate gracefulness of the angelfish is hinted at in this photo of two young angels cruising their domain. Photo by Michael Gilroy.

The dorsal spotting on this wild angelfish is very prominent. Photo by Dr. Herbert R. Axelrod.

After a three/four-day hatching period, the little gray-colored fry emerge with distended bellies caused by the yolk-sac material. This nourishes them for another three/four-day period, during which time they lie about either in small clumps or singly until the sac is absorbed. Eventually they rise up from the bottom and start to school together while searching for food. It is hard to believe that, though only a few days old, they already unite as a flock to start life together.

First food for baby angels, due to their size, is reasonably easy to supply. Even though they appear very tiny to the uninitiated, angel fry are considered fairly large in comparison with the fry of many other tropical fishes. Although they will eat and accept various "infusorians" or forms of microscopic crustacea, newly-hatched brine shrimps are immediately accepted. By following the directions on the package, these shrimps can be hatched out in

24 to 48 hours from eggs purchasable at fish stores or through the mail. Since a brine solution is needed for their hatching the netted little shrimps should be throughly rinsed before using.

To insure proper growth, the bellies of the fry should be kept as full as possible at all times. They should be allowed to eat as much and as often as they desire. As they grow, other foods should be offered, both to vary their diet and to wean them to non-living food substitutes.

Because these methods of heavy feeding to insure fast growth also create a faster build-up of excrement as well as of uneaten foods, both filtration and scavenging fishes should be employed. By use of a filter that uses a piece of plastic foam over the intake filter stem, even the tiniest of free-swimming fry can be assured of filtered water without becoming entrapped. To the filtration should be added frequent partial water changes.

The tiny new fry not only inherit their schooling instinct immediately, but for the first few days they also seek out their spot for the night and lie there in clumps until sunrise of the following day. For this reason no scavenging animals should be employed for at least ten days. If they are introduced too soon and prowl about nocturnally, they often barrel over the clumped fry and eat them.

5.
Diseases

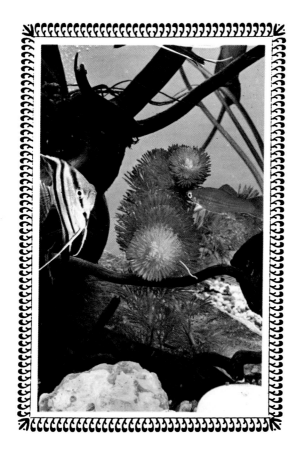

Angelfish are far less susceptible to disease than many of the other species kept by fish hobbyists. Mixed species of fish in an aquarium can often contract a noticeable illness such as "Ich" or white spot disease while angelfish exhibit no signs of this aquatic pestilence.

Above: Angels kept with livebearing species such as the red swordtail shown here will hunt down and eat all of the livebearer babies born in the tank.

Angels are occasionally subject to a form of fin rot, however. It appears as a general lessening of their lengthy finnage to a point where only stumps remain. It frequently starts with other fishes picking at these extra-long appendages, and this picking action causes a definite injury that like any wound, can become fungused. If untreated, the fungus finishes the fin damage even though the attacking fish are removed. The injured fish should be separated from the offenders, and remedial preparations should be put in the aquarium.

Wild-caught individual of Pterophyllum dumerilii. *Photo by Dr. Herbert R. Axelrod.*

Notice the crisply delineated black and silver areas on this half-black angel. Photo by A. Roth.

45

The extreme rounding-over in the pelvic area of this angelfish is not normal.

Fish diseases can appear for several reasons, including the accidental introduction of an already sick fish to the aquarium, or from a traumatic shock brought about by sudden and too drastic changes of temperature, or even by an accident or wound inflicted by another fish.

If symptoms in the form of clamped fins, itching, shimmying, listlessness or loss of appetite are seen, immediate steps should be taken to keep what might be a light case from developing into a serious condition. A good book on fish disease which includes both diagnosis and treatment will be of use to you.

6.
Angelfish varieties

Within the past thirty years, through careful selective breeding, certain morphological changes have been occurring amongst angelfish. As the normal silver angel became more and more inbred, frequent mutations or variants appeared, sometimes as only a single specimen. Separated and crossed back into the strain from which it appeared

This peculiarly patterned angelfish is a mutant from the black lace strain. Photo by Lakeland Fish Hatcheries.

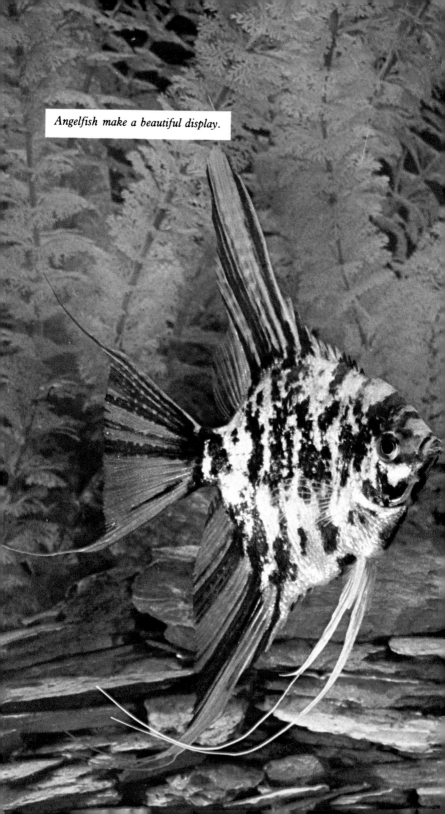

Angelfish make a beautiful display.

or back to another similar-looking fish, new strains have been achieved and established.

From these new strains came still others. Now at least six variations of angelfish are recognized as fairly standard, and at least that number again have been seen and kept, if only for a short time. It is of interest to note that as the variations become more and more fancy, the weaker they are, the more susceptible to disease and the more difficult to breed, especially in quantity.

Without a doubt the greatest sensation that occurred in the hobby came about with the introduction of black angelfish. Because it occurred in the tanks of several fish breeders at approximately the same time, each claimed to

Black angelfish in a display tank. Black angels contrast nicely with brightly colored tropicals. Photo by Gene Wolfsheimer.

Black veil angelfish; black veils rarely exhibit the intensity of black color that can be achieved in a non-veiltail specimen. Photo by Gene Wolfsheimer.

be the first one to breed it. Each claimed to have worked diligently, patiently crossing and re-crossing their own particular breeding stock until, PRESTO, there they were. The facts that the black angelfish came about through constantly breeding black-lace angels to obtain greater and greater darkness, and that these partially dark fish had occurred in Europe but a couple of years before and that it still takes at least eight to nine months to produce a breeding fish, meant very little. In their enthusiasm to lay claim to be black angel originators, the time element was overlooked. Also overlooked, intentionally or not, was the source of their black-lace breeding stock. These fish have varied shading of light gray though almost black in what are normally their silver areas. However, they are not all black specimens.

A letter, loaned to the author by the Lambourne Bros. Tropical Fish Hatchery, dated 'May 25, 1954', from Woolf & Son, Imported and Domestic Tropical Fish, Tampa, Florida, offers both explanation and proof of the true source of the black angelfish:

During the past few years many of our customers have visited us, and with great pride we have shown them our Black Scalares. As a result of 5 years of selected breeding we have finally arrived at a solid black strain, as black as a black molliensia. Unfortunately, they are not very prolific and the strain will not be established and available in sufficient quantities for at least another two years.

As a result of these 5 years of breeding we have accumulated a considerable number of scalares that are not completely black, rather they are colored about the same as a good black tetra.

One of the newest angelfish varieties is the gold crown angel—a white-bodied fish with golden head area. Photo by H. J. Richter.

An angelfish of the variety developed in the mid-1960's and called variously the blushing angelfish and the ghost angelfish. Photo by Dr. Herbert R. Axelrod.

Because of the limited space available in our hatchery, we are going to release these semi-dark scalares to our customers. They will be available in three sizes, medium, large and a few breeding pairs.

There are only a limited number of these available now, and when they are sold there will be practically none available for quite some time...

For those of us in the hobby for a long time the story of Woolf & Son and the black angelfish is well known. Not knowing they were but a generation or so from stock which would give true or high percentage spawnings of all-black fish, these breeders disposed of the black-lace angelfish stock that had backed up on them in quantity. Some of these fish spawned in the aquaria of claimants to the black angel's origin. Voila! Black angelfish...

The following list describes both the better known (Nos. 1-6) and some of the lesser known angelfish variations:

1 The regular Silver Angelfish: The recognized standard in the hobby. A fish of basic clean silver body with crisp black vertical stripes irregularly alternating both in their size and spacing from nose through tail. All fins should be straight, except for long gently-curving ventrals, and of a length considered standard for this species. This is, in fact, the fish upon which other dissimilarities are based and compared.

2 The Black-lace Angelfish: A fish of similar shape and finnage as the silver angel but whose coloring in the light areas tends to darken in gradations from a light silver gray to almost black. However, the silver body is still distinctly visible through its vertical barring.

3 The All-black Angelfish: A fish similar in shape and finnage as Nos. 1 and 2, but whose coloring is *all* black, from nose to ray extensions on the tail. Barring on the body is almost or totally indistinct. Occasionally, in moments of stress or when light penetrates deeply, the vertical barring is very faintly visible.

4 The Silver Veiltail Angelfish: This fish apparently started in Germany from one or more specimens that appeared with unusually lengthy fins. The dorsal and anal as well as the tail are of striking proportions. The very lengthy tail is irregularly ragged at the edge with long filamentous extensions. The coloring of this beautiful variation is quite similar to No. 1, the silver angelfish.

5 The Lace-veil Angelfish: It obviously conforms in finnage to No. 4, the veiltail angel, but its coloration is similar to the description of the lace angelfish, No. 2.

Gold angelfish

6 The All-black Veiltail Angelfish: An all-black fish as described in No. 3, but with the magnificant finnage of the veiltail, No. 4.

7 The Marbled Veiltail Angelfish: Unmarred veiltail finnage, the body markings rearranged to present a very irregular blotchy pattern including some unusual horizontal barring on the tail.

8 The Yellow and Black Angelfish: An exceedingly handsome fish originally appearing with one or two more as a mutant amongst an otherwise set strain of black angels. Its body remains black, but its fins, the dorsal edge of the body, and the head from nose to gill cover are colored a brilliant lemon yellow.

Young black lace angelfish of a very old strain. Photo by Dr. Herbert R. Axelrod.

Black veiltail angelfish. Photo by A. Roth.

9 The All-silver Angelfish: A standard silver angel devoid of its black markings. This makes for an unusual, but not particularly attractive, strain.

10 The Albino Angelfish: Albinism is the partial or complete lack of pigmentation. This fish appears whitish-pink in color with typically albino-pink eyes.

11 The Swallow-tail or Liu Keung Angel: This fantastic variation is named after its breeder in Hong Kong who worked diligently to produce it. So far it has caused mixed emotions amongst dyed-in-the-wool angelfish enthusiasts. Basically, the fish is seen in veiltail forms with lengthy fins and long raggedy tail. Two color variations have been seen, these being the lace and all-black types. Its primary difference is its *double* caudal fin. These gracefully-extended fins (not just one that has been split) are completely separate, both sweeping backward and outward in unison and resembling the tail of a swallow. Just how they happened is still a matter of speculation. It is reasonable to assume that an accidental double-finned specimen from a spawning was pampered to adulthood, where cross-spawnings eventually produced a fish of symmetrical finnage.

There have been reports of many other angelfish variations. A blue fish, a green, a red, a half-black with the
front silver and the back part black, as well as a fish that
is black on one side and light on the other, have all been
recorded. Half-blacks are now fairly well known, and
who knows what tomorrow will bring. If any rules can be
established to bring a semblance of conformity to the
angelfish--rules that will aid in properly judging a truly
quality specimen--they should deal with body and fin
lines.

The body should be as circular as possible. Illustrations
found in very old aquarium literature, usually in the form
of paintings or line drawings, show the first angels in the
hobby to be far more rounded in their silhouette. Certainly not all of these illustrations were as the artist would
have wished the fish to be, but what the first angels

*These two specimens are among the first veiltail angels ever developed. Photo
by Dr. Herbert R. Axelrod.*

This angelfish, bred by Bud Goddard, was one of the first albino angelfish ever produced. Photo by Dr. Herbert R. Axelrod.

(brought into the country long before their present in-bred progeny) really looked like. As for their fins, these have always been vertically straight, with but a gentle backward slope...no bends or grotesque twists or convolutions should ever mar them. If they are displayed in competition, any marring or deformity will definitely detract from points awarded.

Today there are people who think an angelfish with a dorsal fin bent horizontally is a "magnificent specimen"...DON'T YOU BELIEVE IT!

Young angelfish exhibiting a good degree of the "zebra" pattern. Photo by Dr. Herbert R. Axelrod.

Angelfish should have plenty of tankroom for proper development.